UNIVERSITY C

INDEPENDENT STREET ARTS NETWORK

SETTING THE STREETS ALIVE:
A GUIDE TO PRODUCING STREET ARTS EVENTS

PHOTOGRAPHY LIST AND CREDITS

FRONT COVER	Jour de Fete, De La Warr Pavilion, Bexhill – *Maynard Flipflap*
BACK COVER	X.trax, Manchester – *Nutkhut*
PICTURE 01	Slough Arts Alive – *Electric Cabaret*
PICTURE 02	Garden of Delights, Manchester – *Avanti Display*
PICTURE 03	Slough Arts Alive
PICTURE 04	Chelmsford Street Diversions – *Neighbourhood Watch Stilts International*
PICTURE 05a-d	Jour de Fete, De La Warr Pavilion, Bexhill – *Les Grooms*
PICTURE 06	Garden of Delights and X.trax, Manchester – *Chapeau Magique*
PICTURE 07	Stockton International Riverside Festival – *Ojarus*
PICTURE 08	Scharlatan Theater
PICTURE 09	Streets of Brighton – *Kiss Therapy*
PICTURE 10a-c	Slough Arts Alive – *Langley Grammar School and Pearshape Performance*
PICTURE 11	Garden of Delights and X.trax, Manchester – *Cie. de Quatre Saisons*
PICTURE 12	Jour de Fete, De La Warr Pavilion, Bexhill – *The Black Eagles*

Picture front cover	Paul Hewitt
Pictures 1 and 10 a-c	Ray Gibson
Pictures 3, 7, 9 and back cover	Paul Herrmann
Pictures 5 a-d	Jane Freund
Picture 4	Paul Starr
Pictures 2, 6 and 11	Anne and Jane Tucker
Picture 12	Marilyn Kingwell

ISBN 0-9544892-2-5

Published in 2004 by the
Independent Street Arts Network (ISAN)

19 Great Guildford Street,
London SE1 9EZ
UK

Tel: +44 (0) 20 7633 9330
Fax: +44 (0) 20 7261 0014
mail@streetartsnetwork.org.uk
www.streetartsnetwork.org.uk

Distributed by SAM's Books, www.sam-arts.co.uk

Main text Bill Gee, Edward Taylor and Anne Tucker
Case studies Bill Gee, (De La Warr Pavilion) Pam McCrea (Ealing Borough Council), Karen Poley (Zap Art), Liam Rich (Chelmsford Borough Council)
Editor Katy Fuller
Appendices based on examples kindly provided by Manchester International Arts (steward briefing notes) and Newark on Water Festival (audience survey)

Design Tennant Design, Carlisle (01228 514668)
Print Reeds, Penrith, Cumbria (01768 864 214)

Disclaimer As guidance ISAN can accept no responsibility or liability for the application of the information herein contained to specific individual circumstances. This responsibility and liability must continue to lie with the specific event organiser in their local circumstance.

FOREWORD

PICTURE 01   PICTURE 02   PICTURE 03

There is an increasing level of street arts activity in the UK with many producers - often using limited resources - creating events which attract large audiences. These events have an immediacy, where art connects with people in places they use on a daily basis. Much use is made of humour, celebration and spectacle to engage audiences who are often new to the arts. Events are nearly always free and this, alongside the potential for large-scale participation, makes them one of the most readily accessible and inclusive types of art on offer.

Street arts events can be very, very good. They can also be not-so-good, mediocre and occasionally terrible. While some of this can be put down to bad luck, uncontrollable circumstances (the weather for one!), or last minute glitches, much of the responsibility for the success, or otherwise, of an event can be put on the festival producer. Choosing the right work, scheduling it skilfully, knowing your audience, publicising the event and ensuring production and technical aspects run smoothly is no mean feat.

Setting the Streets Alive is designed to steer the reader through the major aspects of presenting street arts on a small to medium scale. This guide is compiled from the collected and expanded materials of one of the Independent Street Arts Network's (ISAN) training programmes, augmented with inspirational case studies from real events. ISAN was established in 2000 when an existing informal network of promoters identified that there was a role for a national strategic organisation to assist in the development of street arts in the UK. ISAN exists to support its membership, but also to contribute to the development of the wider sector and part of this remit includes providing training opportunities and materials for those newer to producing street arts events. This particular training package was initiated because of reports from streets arts companies, through their agents, that the way in which the work was being presented by programmers was sometimes so poor that it was devaluing the work. The source material for this book and the training package were created by Anne Tucker (Manchester International Arts), Edward Taylor (Whalley Range All Stars) and Bill Gee (ISAN and Independent Producer). The guide should be read in conjunction with *Safety Guidance for Street Arts, Carnival, Processions and Large-scale Performances* [1] published in early 2004 by ISAN, which looks in depth at health and safety issues in presenting this form of work.

It is our hope that this book will encourage more people - whether in local authorities, venues, established festivals, regeneration agencies or a host of other organisations which are potential promoters - to work with street arts. It is intended to provide a cushion for those first forays and to ensure that there are consistent standards of professionalism across the country in the role of event producer or promoter. We hope that as well as being a useful first guide, this book will remain an invaluable and inspirational reference point over time.

Bill Gee and Katy Fuller
(ISAN)

[1] See *Further Reading*

CONTENTS

INTRODUCTION

Street arts, seen in many different guises over a fascinating history, exist as an exciting and direct expression of contemporary culture. Encompassing many art forms, street art, as a category, is defined by the arena of presentation. Squares, streets and parks are transformed by the intervention of artists: a building becomes a unique stage set, a shopping centre reveals more than mere consumerism, the streets become more than a means of getting from A to B. Street arts also encourage a move away from the celebrity focus of much popular culture. An audience is drawn in through the talents of experienced artists, rather than superstar names. Out of the planned yet coincidental confrontation of passers-by and street artists, new unforeseen situations arise and these places fill with a transformed atmosphere. At the best events, this atmosphere pervades the area and is infectious, ensuring that the audience becomes part of the festival.

Increasing recognition of not only the breadth of audience that can be brought to these events, but also of the high quality of the work that is presented, means that the current climate is good for artists, producers and audiences. Large-scale and spectacular street arts events, presented as part of the celebrations for the Millennium, the Commonwealth Games, the Queen's Golden Jubilee and the bid for the 2012 London Olympics, have been viewed live by millions and on television by many more and have contributed to the growing public appetite for local activity.

Street arts activity provides cultural opportunities for many people who do not otherwise engage with the professional arts. According to national statistics[2], street arts, circus and carnival events were visited by 23% of the population in 2001. In a national survey jointly undertaken by City University of London and ISAN in 2003[3], 27% of those interviewed never attend other live cultural events, yet 60% of the audience were making a 'special trip' because they knew the event was on and wanted to be there. The majority were between the ages of 20 and 44 with more than a third there with a family group. Perhaps the most significant statistic of all was that over 90% of those interviewed thought street arts a good use of public money and wanted to see more of it.

In recent years there has been a change in culture at Arts Council England (ACE), the Scottish Arts Council and the Department for Culture Media and Sport (DCMS), which reflects the growing realisation of the impact street arts can have on the cultural and social life of an area. Since the publication of their *Strategy on Street Arts* in 2002[4], ACE has made the sector a priority development area and significantly increased their investment, particularly through the Grants for the Arts scheme.

All of these factors and arguments are helping more and more organisations experiment with putting on street arts events in their area. This book guides you through the processes and planning needed to put on a successful event and also points to other sources of reference you will find invaluable. Section 1 starts with the earliest stages of your planning and the decisions to make and relationships to form at this time to ensure a successful event. Section 2 deals with the artistic programme including finding, scheduling and siting the work. Section 3 looks in detail at what will need to be done in the period up to your event including artist liaison, licensing and permissions, technical and production arrangements, health and safety planning and more. Finally, Section 4 deals with the event day itself. The appendices provide useful documents for you to refer to over the course of your planning. We wanted to provide inspirational as well as practical information and we trust this will be found in the four different case studies that have been written up by the organisers of these events.

[2]See research report - *Arts in England: Attendance, Participation & Attitudes in 2001* (Arts Council England, 2002) ISBN. 0-7287089-3-0. Available to download on www.artscouncil.org.uk
[3]Findings published by ISAN in 2004. To obtain a copy, contact mail@streetartsnetwork.org.uk
[4]See *Further Reading*

GETTING STARTED

THE FIRST DECISIONS – DATE, STRUCTURE, AUDIENCE, LOCATION

Before you can begin to plan out your event in detail, some very fundamental decisions need to be made. The four corners of your event will be formed by your decisions on the four variables of date, structure, audience and location. While some of these will, most likely, be fixed for you, there will still be decisions to make to ensure the most successful event. The four different elements all interrelate and inform each other in the decision making process. The sections below discuss some of the factors that might influence your decisions on these areas.

Date
→ Which season?
→ Tying in with other events and celebrations or avoiding a clash with them?
→ Term-time or school holidays?
→ Bank holiday weekends?

Most street arts events take place in the summer - for reasons primarily to do with climate and the likelihood of rain or snow - with a calendar of events concentrated in the period from May to September. That said, there are street events which take place annually in the winter and significant dates such as New Year, November 5th, Diwali and others that play their part in the street arts calendar.

It may be that your event has been initiated to tie in with other celebrations, such as those mentioned above, a one-off national event, for example the Golden Jubilee, or a one-off local event, such as the opening of a newly pedestrianised street. On a local level it is important to think of traditional dates for events such as community fairs or other exhibitions and local church, mosque or temple festivals and usage. It may be that you see an advantage in coinciding with such events. However, if this is the case then it is important to build this into your plans. On the other hand, if your event stands alone, you don't want to risk losing its impact by, for example, programming it on St Patrick's Day, when it is unrelated to the festivities. These clashes are possible on a local or national level. In the example of sports fixtures, an important match on a local football pitch could cause havoc for parking, traffic and the sheer number of people on the streets. Equally, a match in a town far away can severely affect your audience numbers and profile... if it is the FA cup final or an important World Cup qualifier!

Do consider whether you want to put your event within term-time or school holidays as you will attract a slightly different audience depending on your choice. When it comes to participatory activities, you will need to consider whether you wish to work through the statutory sector, e.g. schools, or the voluntary sector, for example playschemes or carers' / family groups and plan the timing of your event accordingly. Do remember, however, that it is not only schools that operate on term-times, but also some other groups and organisations, such as community dance / drama groups. As ever, research your local situation carefully.

Be wary of what you are pitting yourself against when programming on a bank holiday. Check out other local events and traditions before you commit. Is your town already somewhere that attracts people anyway on a long weekend? If so you could be an asset to the town's tourism strategy.

Timing / structure
→ A one day afternoon event (Saturday or Sunday)
→ An evening event beginning at dusk
→ Both daytime and evening, e.g., running from midday through to midnight.
→ A weekend-long programme
→ A programme spread over a number of days, weekends or even weeks

Your budget will inevitably be a major factor in determining the length of the event you go for. Street arts often benefit from being presented en masse and the effect can be seriously diminished if the work has to be spread thinly to last over an extended period.

The advantage of a one day event is that you can, at a push, manage the majority of the get-in and get-out on the same day or evening before, thus avoiding or lessening the issue of overnight security for guarding temporary art works and equipment. Working over several weekends is often only financially practical if much of the infrastructure is permanently in place.

Street arts can have spectacular impact at night with many street arts companies producing work with projection, fire, pyrotechnics and sophisticated lighting. Working at night does incur additional costs in lighting and security however. Other considerations with dusk or night-time events include whether there is adequate provision of public transport and toilets, whether local residents may be disturbed by noise and whether you will be able to attract an audience at that time. Families may be reluctant to stay out too late in certain areas. It is interesting to note that this can be the very reason for putting on an event and reclaiming their right to feel safe in that space.

Think of the logistics of the start time and the implications this may have for additional hotel costs for artists you will be working with. Depending upon where your event location is, an afternoon start will probably mean that many of the artists will be able to travel that morning. You also need to consider local businesses and their opening times. The event may well be beneficial to certain businesses (e.g., cafés, bars etc), but be aware that others may feel differently about the event. Liaison with businesses, shops, cafés and bars in the festival areas is vital. Arrange performances at times and in places which do not disrupt shopping entrances or church services and which make the most of late night shopping and other retail promotions.

For more tips on how to programme the work within your chosen structure...
See *PROGRAMMING: Putting Together a Programme and Scheduling the Work.*

Audience
→   All ages?
→   Children / young people / older people?
→   Families?
→   Particular communities?
→   Difficult to access groups?

Street arts events are very successful in attracting an audience of people who do not usually participate in cultural activities such as going to the theatre. In the ISAN/City University research, 27% of those interviewed never went to other professional cultural provision. The question you are most likely to be concerned with is how to access the audiences you have planned the event for; how to attract them to your event and give them a good time once they are there. The key elements - what you programme for the event, how you market this and the timings you decide on - will influence who comes.

It is possible to programme street arts that will appeal to a very broad audience. Be wary, however, of programming a swathe of acts that purport to have "broad appeal". So often this equates to not quite doing it for anyone and with the wealth and quality small-scale performance available, it can be better to aim to programme specific individual acts that will appeal to different sections of the audience you are expecting.

Be aware of the community you are working in. As you are putting something on in a public space, it is sensible and respectful to think about the residents and users of that space. Are there particular communities that may not feel as if the event is for them? Do you need to produce publicity in languages other than English? Can you provide participatory elements to introduce groups to the event and give them some ownership of it? Can you ensure you will make the event as interesting, accessible and safe as possible for audience members with sensory impairments and physical disabilities?

For more information on attracting your audience...
See *MAKING IT HAPPEN: Marketing and Press*

Location
→   Town / city centre streets
→   A purpose built performance space or public square
→   A park
→   Single-site
→   Multiple-sites
→   Shifting location, i.e. with a procession or parade

This is what it's all about - freeing yourself from the constraints of a theatre space or gallery and getting creative with the place itself. Street arts events do not have to take place in the street, although this is often where they work best. Town centre festivals have an immediacy and, despite your best efforts to publicise the event, there will still be those who stumble across your artistic intervention while innocently popping into town for a look at the shoe shops. This unwitting audience will provide some of the more hilarious reactions of the day! If you do use a town centre location, investigate carefully how you can work with pedestrianised areas and public squares.

Parks can also be a successful location for street arts and provide a traffic-free, manageable location. If you intend to gate and ticket the event this can be considerably easier in a park than on the streets. You may have to work harder to draw an audience specifically to a park for an event, but as parks are traditional places of leisure an audience does seem able to commit itself more readily to a show than in a busy street.

Processions and parades are celebratory and provide an excellent opportunity for participation. They can be used to draw an audience to a particular location, such as a park, for further performance. Routes can be difficult to plan and it is essential to work closely with external organisations, such as the police and highways.

Street arts can also include site specific work, created for a particular location. The type of event we are looking at here is unlikely to have the budget to commission site specific work, so it is not covered in any depth in this guide. The same is also true of touring large scale or spectacular performance the budgets for which are likely to be well in excess of £30,000.

For more information on how to site your performances within your chosen location…
See PROGRAMMING: Siting the Work.

FUNDRAISING AND BUDGETING
FUNDRAISING AND FUNDING SOURCES
Street arts events are normally presented as 'free to view' for audiences. However you do need to be aware - and make sure others are aware - that to do these events properly is a costly (but well worthwhile) investment.

You will have to be prepared to do some detective work to find out who is likely to fund either the whole, or particular elements, of your event. Where possible it is sensible, if not necessary, to have a range of funders, so that if problems arise with one source of funding, it

is not the event in its entirety that is jeopardised. Coupled with this, you should devise a series of plans that relate to the different scenarios you might face depending on the success of your fundraising. This way, you have, as far as possible, contingencies to fall back on.

In 2001 ISAN undertook an in-depth review of funding sources for street arts at that time, looking at both promoters' and artists' income sources. Local authorities were the principal investors at that time, with almost 50% of the income coming from this source. What follows is an updated list.

Funding Sources for Street Arts
→ Local Authorities (Town, District, Metropolitan and County Councils)
  - Arts, heritage, tourism, leisure and community development departments
  - Economic development, city/town centre management and markets and fairs
  - Health and social services
  - Regeneration agencies
  - Single regeneration budgets
  - Training agencies
→ European Union
  - European Regional Development Funds
  - Structural funds to counter demise of traditional industries
  - Interreg. to foster closer links between borders
→ Commercial
  - Diverse sponsorship sources including leisure, travel, telecommunications, new technology and property companies
  - Shopping centres
→ Arts funding system
  - National Arts Councils
  - British Council
→ Arts venues' existing budgets
→ Arts festivals' existing budgets
→ Trusts and Foundations
→ Education (schools, colleges, Universities and increasingly Creative Partnerships)
→ Box Office
  - where events charge for entry to a site where street arts are being presented

BUDGETING
The main difference when budgeting for street arts and outdoor performances is to remember that production costs may be high. You will have to bring in much of any necessary infrastructure and staffing for the event, whereas if you are running an arts centre or theatre year round, many of these costs disappear into large annual budgets rather than specific event budgets.

As a very rough guide to budgeting for an event, you should allow:

10 - 15%	for marketing,
10 - 15%	for staffing/stewards etc and
15 - 25%	on production costs (stages, lighting, security, PAs, barriers etc.)
45 - 65%	on artistic programme

Don't forget expenditure such as

licenses, insurance and costs relating to Health and Safety measures.

Artists and companies may present you with an all-in cost and will provide for their own technical needs and transport as well as cover their fees from this. Others may quote you a fee and then ask you to provide any other requirements - equipment, accommodation and so on - on top of this. You also need to find out what you can expect for your fee, such as whether a performance will take place several times over the day

For multi-site small scale work, you can calculate roughly what possibilities you have. Working on anything between £400 and £900 per street show and £700 per band, and giving approximately 90 minutes overall performance time (eg. 2 x 45 mins or 3 x 30 mins) per group, you can plot very quickly how many sites and hours you can run for your budget. Of course these figures are only a guide to be used at the earliest planning stages. It is often worthwhile programming a company that may present a particularly visually stunning show which will cost more than this budget guide, particularly if they have good promotional imagery which you could use to market the whole event. The same applies to an international company who are special enough for a local paper or radio station to take particular interest in.

Once you have an idea of your overall budget you can begin to work out what you can reasonably expect for your money, which you will then be able to relate back to your plan for the event. Remember, if you are short on programming money, it may well be better to shorten the overall length of the event and be sure of still providing impact.

For further examples of who funds these events and how the money is spent...
See the *Case Studies*

INITIAL CONSULTATION
Early on in your planning you will need to do some consultation to be sure that you will be able to go ahead.

Groups and individuals you may be advised to form a relationship with at this stage are:
→ Police
→ Licensing department, Local Authority
→ Highways department, Local Authority
→ Town Centre / Park Managers
→ Retailers
→ Other culture providers in the locality – theatres, galleries, community arts projects, etc.

If you are in the lucky position of having access to production manager support or have a friendly health and safety officer in your organisation then do make friends with them and try to gain some guaranteed time that they can spend on the project in the months before the event.

Creating a small team that looks at production and logistical issues is often a good model to adopt. As well as the advantage of a number of heads and different experiences being better than one, it is likely that creating a small team that meets regularly for 3 or 4 months may well assist in developing a shared sense of ownership for the event. However, do remember it is your event and do not let it get hijacked by someone else's agenda or commercial interest. Stick with your vision, as it can always be reviewed for the following year.

You will also begin to build up reciprocal relationships with the members of this group. Being able to make clear arguments about the benefits of your event, as relevant to each party, should help you form alliances. In the arts we are often more used to making the social and cultural arguments, but don't forget about the economic benefits as well, such as for local businesses.

Remember, however, that it is not always the case that a street arts event which draws a large crowd to a town centre will necessarily result in an increase in local traders' takings that day. It may be that you have programmed such amazing work that the audience actually stay out of the shops (except for cafés, sandwich shops, etc.). However, what has been found is that such an experience can change the perception about the town centre and what a good environment it has and can encourage people to return for shopping more frequently in the future. Town centre managers should be very receptive to this argument.

CASE STUDY 1: CHELMSFORD STREET DIVERSIONS
Liam Rich, Chelmsford Borough Council Special Events Team

THE EVENT

Chelmsford Street Diversions was established in 2003 by Chelmsford Borough Council Special Events Team. It was recognised that there was a gap in the events programme for something taking place within the town centre itself. The main street is pedestrianised and lends itself well to street arts, so it was decided to use this artform, and the burgeoning British scene in particular, to animate the town centre and create an atmosphere where the seemingly normal might turn into a quirky, comedic situation.

The programme runs for three days and is made up of smaller scale walkabout and some larger scale work. The walkabout acts have been chosen to show the oddity that can emerge from the familiar, as exemplified in the work of companies such as the Natural Theatre Company, the idea being to engage the audience by making them do a double-take. This smaller scale, more intimate approach is then contrasted with one or two, bigger impact, unignorable, pieces, such as Neighbourhood Watch Stilts International's caterpillar. The focus is definitely on performance and entertainment, mainly because Street Diversions is produced by the Events Team. There is also an Arts Education Team who deliver workshops and participatory activities in other contexts, but the event itself tends to stick to professional work to achieve the impact desired and not dilute the budget available through other activities.

The programme runs only during the daytime, which means that work is concentrated into a few hours each day, allowing for a bigger impact. It also keeps production costs lower to work only in the daylight. Without a lot of investment and careful planning it would be inappropriate, in any case, to run street arts activities at night time in the town centre. Like many towns across Britain, night time leisure activities revolve mainly around bars, clubs and alcohol and the atmosphere could be difficult to manage for the kinds of performance the festival wants to programme.

The audience response to the festival has been overwhelmingly positive with approximately 85% of people who returned a feedback postcard rating the event highly. It also succeeds in attracting an audience from outside the town.

THE LOCAL SITUATION

For 15 years, the events team has run Chelmsford Spectacular, which consists of three outdoor evening concerts and a daytime event with an audience of 40,000. The success of this event and its time honoured relationships with local organisations means that there has also been support for the new event, Street Diversions, from the beginning. This was particularly apparent with the local radio and newspapers.

Other welcome support has come from the two shopping centres in the vicinity of the performance site, which both gave some financial support to the event. The Council's Town Centre Manager works on involving local businesses in all the events produced. Disappointingly, the bigger chain stores, which make up the majority of the high street businesses, are often difficult to involve, with much coming down to how far a particular manager is prepared to address local concerns over the larger national directives that can stifle this. It would be a great step forward for the street arts sector if it could encourage investment and support from the big names that often provide the dominant backdrop for the performance.

BUDGET BREAKDOWN

Income - where does the money come from?
Overall budget approx £28,000
→   just over half of this from Arts Council England
→   £12,000 from the events team's core budget
→   two local shopping centres gave approx £500 each

Expenditure - where does it go?	%
→ artistic programme;	80
→ technical / production;	<5
→ staffing;	<5
→ marketing.	10

Production costs are very low because there were no stages, the PA needed was borrowed and the smaller acts provided for their own technical needs. Staffing costs are low as there is a core events team already. The only costs are for bringing in some stewards.

WHY DOES IT WORK?

The programming of the acts is undertaken with great care to achieve the desired effect. Choosing to focus on performance, rather than also trying to provide community workshops on this scale of budget, means that a lot of the budget can be given over to artists fees and the volume of performance is high enough to make a big impact. There is a good balance of the subtle work and more "in-your-face" high drama. This diversity hangs together well, however, to create an overall theme of quirky, surprising entertainment. The marketing is also carefully managed to help establish beforehand the sense that the event offers something new and exciting.

As seems to frequently be the case with street arts events, the tenacity of one or two people is the main reason that the event goes ahead and is as successful as it is. It can be a struggle to persuade others until they have seen the evidence, but it is worth sticking to your guns.

This year (2004), it was also no small issue (but a great wonder!) that the rain started on the dot of 4pm Sunday; the time the festival finished!

PICTURE 04

PROGRAMMING

KNOWLEDGE OF THE WORK

Programming is the fun and creative part of the job. A good programme relies on the quality of each of its individual components and it is your responsibility to know that they are good. Your tastes will obviously come into play, while you will always be considering what will appeal to your audience. The wide range of available work means that there will be something to fit the context of your event. Remember that an event that has been presenting street arts for some time will have built up a knowledge of the work with its audience and may, therefore, programme differently from a newer event.

This guide cannot provide an overview of what work is out there and cannot even give a description of all the types of work that are creatively imagined and produced by dedicated street arts practitioners up and down the country. Whether it is dance work choreographed within costumes of air-conditioning ducting; theatre inside a box which is lowered onto your head; storytelling inside an inflatable whale; an aerialist dangling from beneath an helium filled balloon; a band of bellboys armed with nothing more than brass instruments; a kathak dance choreographed for grand staircases or two acrobats with sparklers up their asses, it all is part of the rich tapestry of what street arts can be. The photographic images in this guide have been specially selected partly to demonstrate this incredible range.

Knowledge of the work is paramount. The best way to find good work that will suit your needs is to go out and see the companies in action and this means that the trips to showcases and other festivals are worth their weight in gold. The majority of the festivals and major programmers of street arts in the UK and the dates of their events are listed on the ISAN website which is regularly updated. ISAN also compiles and distributes a monthly bulletin during the summer months giving details of forthcoming events. You can register for this through the website whether or not you are a member.

Showcase festivals are particularly set up to act as a marketplace for the sector. Promoters who attend can see many (often 50 plus) companies over a couple of days and are provided with contact information on all the companies. Sometimes companies present their work just for expenses on the expectation that they will be able to recoup their outlay from subsequent bookings they receive. The major UK showcase festivals are

Streets of Brighton	www.zapuk.com
2nd weekend in May	
Xtrax, Manchester	www.xtrax.org.uk
1st weekend in June	

The directories that both these events produce are an excellent research resource.

In addition there are a number of major international showcase festivals in Europe which are all listed on the ISAN website.

Agencies such as Fools Paradise, Missing Link, Plush, Crowd Pullers and Continental Drifts are often a useful source for a number of companies who will be listed on their websites or in the annual brochures they produce. Fools Paradise present a showcase of some of their acts early in the New Year. However, the downfall of this is that the work is presented indoors to a room full of promoters without many members of the general public to respond in a normal fashion! You may of course find that if you go down an agency route some of the fun is taken out of the process for you, but they often provide a good service in terms of publicity materials and the contracting process.

It may be worth your while enquiring at your regional Arts Council office as to whether they have any lists of street arts specific companies in your own region. If you are near other regions then do extend this search to the neighbouring areas. In some regions such as Yorkshire, Bristol and the North West there are regional networks of artists and promoters.

Do not be afraid to ask colleagues in your own professional networks. It is vital that promoters discuss work that they have seen with each other and assess the qualities that may make a particular show perfect for a particular location. Openness and a willingness to constructively develop a critical language will only help the development of the sector in the coming years; of course ensuring the discourse is extended to the artists. ISAN members actively work to develop the sector by sharing their information. This includes sharing event dates early on and programming collaboratively to produce tours for international companies, thereby cutting costs. ISAN meetings also offer networking opportunities where discussion of work seen can take place informally.

Speak to artists and find out what work they are developing and what has been touring successfully for a while. If a group that you are confident in has a repertoire, there could be some sort of discussion about which show would be most suitable for your event.

PUTTING TOGETHER A PROGRAMME

There is a lot of flexibility in putting together a programme of street arts and much will come down to the individual circumstances and budget. Consider whether you want to mix community elements and local amateur performers with the professional groups that you are booking and how to do this successfully, so that the event is a suitable platform for both. This will depend upon many factors, perhaps the most important being how many collaborating partners you could muster to be part of the project. If you had a major arts in education or Creative Partnerships programme and they buy into being a partner for activities in the period leading up to the event, then a significant young people's input is likely. If your proposed site includes a river or canal it may be that the Environment Agency or British Waterways Board would work with you to develop a range of complimentary water related activities.

Some suggestions follow for the programming mix you might choose for different types of event, but again, use your own judgement and visit other events to see what works well.

For a multi-site high energy afternoon:
→ choose mostly small scale shows - a mixture of static street theatre and circus - a music stage if you think it will be a genuine draw and strolling shows to link the sites. The more amplified shows you have the further apart you need to put them.
→ concentrate the densest part of the programme around the middle of the event and programme more sparsely at the beginning and the end.

→ try and avoid 'ghettoising' any areas e.g., a 'community' stage, or a 'youth' area. It is much more successful to make your audience move around to find what they want - they do!
→ even though street performers are skilled at building audiences, if you are worried about people staying, it may be worth programming shows back to back, so spaces are never left empty requiring the next show to have to pull a crowd. Be conscious of the atmosphere dropping on the day and if it is take remedial action by shifting timings if possible.

For an evening event with warm-up:
→ start gently and build in intensity to the finale (which may be fireworks).
→ try and imagine that some families with children may leave by 9.30pm, so make sure a strong family show happens before then, so they can leave satisfied.
→ you may want to programme a stand alone event without any warm-up, if you think it is worth concentrating your budget. This is likely if the event needs to be at night in summer time (it doesn't get dark till 10.45pm midsummer in central Scotland, 10.15pm in N England and 10.00pm in S England). Recent fireworks legislation has made it now illegal to fire pyrotechnics after 11pm (apart from New Years Eve) so things will get tricky!

For a carnival parade ending in a park
→ encourage community involvement through collaborations with carnival artists - samba musicians, costume makers and dancers.
→ explore exchanges with other community carnivals to build up sections of your procession and to give your participants the chance to partake in other carnivals around the country.
→ invite experienced Mas bands from elsewhere to take part. Many will relish the chance to showcase their costumes at another event (but will need expenses covering).

→ make sure that all people watching the parade are encouraged and have space in the parade to join in and follow to the park.

→ programme some performance in the park while the procession is on the road, for those who do not follow the parade, but come straight to the site.

→ make sure there is a high level of very visual and loud activity scheduled for the time when the parade and the audience is due to arrive in the park so people know it is a place to enter and stay.

→ make sure the people who have just paraded have their own area to go to change, which is away from the main public area.

→ encourage people to bring picnics and designate a picnic area for this

→ the marketing needs to have been really clear about the timing and structure of the event.

SCHEDULING THE WORK

A good programmer needs to be able to sensitively schedule their programme to ensure the best results from the performers and the best experience for the audience. Scheduling and siting the work (see below) go hand in hand. At an early stage draw up a spreadsheet with the different sites and the different areas that you may want to site walkabout performers and make an initial draft of what the programme could be. If you have a number of highlight acts in the programme you may want these to have a dedicated space within the schedule. Remember many performers will present two or even three performances or walkabout sessions in one day. It is likely that over the weeks and months reasons will present themselves why you should make changes to this schedule. Be flexible and keep everyone – especially performers – informed of any changes.

Consider how to

→ programme an event so it flows well and builds to a climax, or ebbs and flows to suit the times of day people use your town centre.

→ timetable shows so you avoid crushpoints or overcrowding in some places at particular times.

→ present shows so as to avoid noise clashes or parading artists marching through fixed show sites

→ ensure the right balance of artforms and styles and to know that noise levels, timings (so that shows can run back to back) and set-up arrangements can all be managed.

→ be sensitive to climate, e.g., planning carefully in winter so people move around sufficiently so they don't get too cold; thinking about possible wet weather provision; considering where a strong summer sun may be shining – into the eyes of artists or audience is not ideal.

SITING THE WORK

Visit your site/s enough times early on that you become sensitive to the physical spaces available and what they offer. This includes appraisal of:

→ sightlines, slopes, backdrop walls, fences or bushes

→ the proximity to dangerous or noisy traffic flow

→ the size of crowd that can be contained there

→ shops and other buildings that may require access

Using a variety of sites makes for an interesting event and allows you to accommodate different kinds of work. Think about street corners, natural slopes, stages if necessary, and purpose built performance areas. Remember that artists will need access to dressing room facilities, refreshments and vehicle parking not a million miles from where they are performing. Also, if you are thinking of a slightly unconventional site, remember to consult the artists first.

If you have a number of sites running at the same time for performance these need to be far enough apart that there is not a split in focus for the audience in deciding which one to watch. In these different spaces it is good, obviously, not to programme similar work at the same time. You also need to be aware of visual or sound pollution between the different sites of a multi-site event. You should also assess this in relation to local shops and avoid putting a site near shops with loud noise. Equally, if you will be using a powerful PA you need to check with the shops whether outside noise is OK. This must be done well in advance.

Some spaces will be where different specific groups hang out and it can be best to avoid using these spaces. Whether they be young people or alcoholics, it gives the space a particular sense of ownership, and the usual 'owners' can make your life difficult. It is important that these issues are identified early in the planning process and strategies thought through to deal with them. Alcoholics can be unpredictable and subject to major shifts in their responses. Teenagers are usually best drawn in from the outside, rather than through an attempt to invade their space.

Areas outside pubs and bars can be difficult as those seated at tables may not be seated there to watch a show but for their own entertainment and with the added factor of alcohol an interaction between street show and these people can get aggressive or challenging. If you need to use it, this sort of vicinity may be a more appropriate location for a small music stage.

Some spaces have their regular buskers and beggars. This is tricky as professional groups are aware (and sympathetic) of the fact that these people are doing this to scrape a living. Commandeering somebody else's "pitch" may cause resentment and division. If alternative spaces can be found that are equally as good, then everyone's happy. Otherwise you can talk to the buskers to try and find an amicable solution - they may well accept your case. If the town centre has a licensed buskers policy, it is important to liaise with whoever coordinates this in advance and potentially to block that day out for other licensed busking.

You must check whether the space is used by lorries/vans delivering to local businesses. One rogue lorry can add to a show (unless the group has a fixed set) but constant disruption can have a detrimental effect on a whole programme.

Static performances need space to work in and will specify how big or small this is in their technical information. These sites are best if they are just to one side of the regular thoroughfare - too far and it will be difficult to lure people, too near and people will walk through

the show. If the show is about continuous improvisation with the public the latter may be better, but you need to check this with the company concerned.

Spaces in front of benches look ideal but can be difficult. A group likes to build up an audience who specifically want to see the show. If people are sitting down already, they may not be there for the show and will not help the atmosphere. Once a Briton has decided they are NOT going to look, the results may become quite hilarious but can also be dispiriting to the performers' energies.

Some companies like a back wall and to play on three sides, others like to play in the round.

Points to remember while programming:
→ travel costs
→ accommodation needs for artists coming from far or working late at night
→ dressing rooms and refreshments for artists
→ parking for artists (and the public)
→ vehicle access to some sites for unloading props and sets - stewards to mind these while artists park, change, eat and rest between shows
→ strolling groups need a steward to accompany them. Be aware of any other steward needs groups may have
→ trees have leaves on them in summer (you may be doing site visits in winter) and sightlines may therefore be very different
→ space for audiences to stand that does not block shop entrances or spill into the road
→ space for queues to form at booth shows (as above)
→ bands need changeover time, so if you want to keep the site alive programme acoustic floor shows in between sets

CASE STUDY 2: JOUR DE FÊTE, DE LA WARR PAVILION, BEXHILL
Bill Gee, Jour de Fête Programmer DLWP, Bexhill

THE EVENT

The De La Warr Pavilion (DLWP) is a Grade 1 listed Modernist building, which is a multi-artform venue situated on the sea front in Bexhill on the South Coast of England. The Jour de Fête Festival has been presented in, around and on the DLWP since its first edition in 2000. Despite the DLWP being fully closed for an extensive refurbishment throughout 2004, a two-day festival on the August bank holiday weekend was staged on the surrounding lawns and promenade, maintaining continuity for the loyal and growing audience for what has become a very important part of the Bexhill summer. In previous years a 4 to 8 week programme has taken place in the weeks building up to the finale weekend.

The range of work presented in Jour de Fête has been broad, from a range of visual, performative installations by UK and international companies such as Stan's Café; Les Cubitenistes and the Whalley Range All Stars, to high quality skill-based shows from companies such as Mimbre; Aristobulle and Boni and Caroli; broad range music programming from North African Rai to Brass Bands from Rye and classic small-scale shows from many companies including Avanti Display, Strangelings, Desperate Men and Batchata.

The different shows have found homes outside, either on the rear terrace or grass lawns. One year, the indoor 1000 seat theatre space was emptied to create an outdoor-style space inside, bringing this kind of activity to the interior of the building, which is usually programmed in a very different style.

Jour de Fête includes a finale show on a larger scale to add focus and impact to the event. For the last three years this has been through a commissioning collaboration between Bexhill and two other festivals - Bracknell and Newark-on-Water - which has secured investment from Arts Council England each year. In previous years, operating on a more modest budget, the event still managed to programme finale performances, including *Reve d'Herbert* (Cie. Quidams and Inko'nito) in 2000, which proved a great and gentle introduction for an audience of c800 people that year to have a first taste of work of scale. In subsequent years, work by sculptor and pyrotechnician Denis Tricot; World Famous and Peepolykus; Walk the Plank and Mark Murphy has seen a growth in the audience to c3000 for this Sunday evening special moment.

THE LOCAL SITUATION

Over the 5-year period the Jour de Fête programme has been a key audience development tool for the DLWP in helping to build the family audience, not just for performances and events but also for their casual recreational use of this remarkable building; there is a hope that the programme will attract people and they will continue to come back. The building's key feature is that it is a place of leisure and recreation and with its sea hugging position people often are more at ease within themselves than in the hustle and bustle of a street setting. The audience is now composed of a significant core group of Jour de Fête fans who have developed a real taste for the unexpected and challenging. These are people drawn to specific acts and those just drawn to the building. It genuinely is an audience that spans all ages and many multi-generational family groups are regular attenders.

There are many advantages to a building producing such an event, including having an existing staff team to cover areas such as technical, logistics, health and safety, marketing, PR, and even artist catering.

Though the event is led very much by the artistic vision of the DLWP there are also a number of important local stakeholders – Rother District Council; the Coastal Currents sub-regional festival; the Town Centre Action Group; Youth Services and their music development project.

Active engagement with local people has been an important strand of the programme from siting performance artist Caroline Amoros in the town for a week creating a photo document of the moments of shared interaction, to a Red Earth project seeing the creation of 200 wish flags (later ceremonially burnt on the beach) and from a local brass band being integrated into new commissions, to local young bands being spotlighted for the first time.

BUDGET BREAKDOWN

Income - where does the money come from?
The street arts programme, as described above, costs about £30,000 to put on. It may be interesting for readers to note that the total budget, however, is around £90,000, - £60,000 of this going towards the commissioning of the finale piece.

The festival is funded from core DLWP investment that in turn comes from:
→ ACE
→ Rother District Council
→ East Sussex County Council

Other project investment has been secured from
→ Town Centre Action Group
→ ACE
→ PRS Foundation
→ Local retailers

Expenditure - where does it go?	%
→ artistic programme;	50
→ technical / production;	20
→ staffing;	15
→ marketing.	15

WHY DOES IT WORK?

It works due to a fantastic setting which is already a place of leisure, a committed audience, an adventurous artistic programme, regularity through the years, staff who have gained a high regard for the work, a local paper that both previews and intelligently reviews work and a well informed programmer.

PICTURE 05a

PICTURE 05b

PICTURE 05c

PICTURE 05d

MAKING IT HAPPEN

ROLES – WHO DOES WHAT?

A street arts event can be incredibly complex and require a number of skilled personnel who are knowledgeable, patient and flexible. Some of the key roles are outlined in the list below, while the following section further explores the tasks that need to be carried out by you and your team. Of course, having an individual person to fulfil each of these roles would be an untold luxury for most smaller scale events. Staff members working solely on, for example, marketing or fundraising can often be out of the question. Some roles, such as that of community worker, are more pertinent to certain events than others. One person may take on more than one of these roles, but it is a good idea to be clear about what the different responsibilities of each are.

→ Director / Programmer – essentially the decision maker for the event. Some events will split this role between the artistic side (director or programmer) and the overall production side (producer).
→ Programme Coordinator - the person who will put all necessary elements in place for the programme to go ahead, eg. artist liaison and contracting.
→ Production Manager – taking care of the technical and operations side of things, such as creating a site plan, hiring in any staging and equipment, generators and barriers, planning and booking stewards.
→ Health and Safety Officer – devising and implementing the Safety Plan and liaising with the necessary authorities.
→ Marketing / Press Officer
→ Fundraiser (often Director/Programmer)
→ Community / Outreach Worker.

CONTRACTS AND ARTIST LIAISON

Contract all artists as early as possible. Their contract should include:
→ all monies you are paying - travel costs, fees, per diems
→ any provision of accommodation
→ any provision of equipment
→ your requirements from them e.g., proof of insurance, technical specification
→ cancellation terms
→ terms if the group is unable to perform (e.g. due to adverse weather)

If possible, it is good for a promoter to agree a simple contract with their lawyer or legal department so that it covers all the bases but does not result in a weighty tome being sent out with so many pages of clauses and sub-clauses that an artist needs a lawyer themselves to check it through. In practice most elements of a contract are agreed on the phone and via email. It is vital in your negotiations with an artist to be clear at what stage the discussions are at. Though everyone has their own terms a useful guide would be:

→ Initial enquiry – availability, price and technical requirements discussed – no commitment of either party
→ Provisional – price, date and requirements agreed and date held. Normally an agreement is then made that this will remain like this for a set period (maybe a month) to allow for such things as confirmation of site or funding on which the booking is dependant. If in this period anything changes for the promoter they should immediately inform the artist. Equally if a different offer comes in for the artist they need to inform the promoter and probably give them a reduced time period – maybe 48 hours to confirm or not.
→ Confirmed subject to contract. When this happens it is advisable to move to contract stage as quickly as possible. There are few things that should get in the way at contract stage unless additional areas come out from either party not previously discussed. Do not agree to two different contracts i.e., an artist's and your own.

Artists also need to be provided with clear instructions and maps (not faxed versions of photocopies, or email attachments) showing where and when they should arrive, where they can park, a reception point and who they are going to meet. These need to arrive at least two weeks in advance. Many groups are away touring right up to the gig

so don't return home to pick up mail. It is always useful to include a mobile phone number for artists to contact if they are lost or in difficulties.

Artists should provide a clear technical specification that your production manager should see early on. The contract should have formalised who will be providing what equipment and so on. You may need to ask artists to provide a risk assessment for their show to feed into your overall safety planning. Ask artists to send invoices in advance and pay them by cheque on the day where possible.

ISAN member organisations sign up to a code of practice pertaining to the engagement of artists. ISAN also operates a conciliation process for artists who have had a problematic experience with one of the member organisations. Further details can be found on the ISAN website. From 2005 the intention is that ISAN members will have a clause in their contracts that makes the Code of Practice and conciliation process explicit.

For an example contract for artists…
See *APPENDIX 1*

HEALTH AND SAFETY PLANNING

Health and safety planning for events of this nature is paramount and while it can be complex, it is manageable. ISAN's publication Safety Guidance for Street Arts, Carnival, Processions and Large-Scale Performances offers comprehensive advice on this area and includes case studies of different types of event and example risk assessments. The other key document that event producers rely on is *The Event Safety Guide* (The Purple Book) produced by the Health and Safety Executive. A brief outline of some of the main considerations is given below, but both of these documents should be referred to for more detail. [5]

SAFETY PLAN

You will need to produce an event safety plan that covers a range of emergencies (though in 99% of cases you will never need to use this). You need to describe the nature of the event, the probable flow of people, where crushes might build up, which roads might need to be crossed if there is a parade and any potentially dangerous elements e.g., fireworks, electricity, things that can fall over or from height and injure artists or public. You will need to meet with the council safety officers at least once during planning time. A safety planning group may include representatives from the police, fire, highways (traffic), environmental health (food safety, noise, other nuisance) and there may be others - city engineers, street lighting etc. - depending on the event. It is advisable to have one meeting early on to give them your outline plans and ask them for feedback on any particular areas of possible concern they think you should focus on. A second meeting should follow once you have your full safety plan.

RISK ASSESSMENT

It is necessary to produce a risk assessment for the event as a whole which includes the specific components within it. If you are working within a local authority it is likely that you will have a Safety Officer who should be able to guide you through this process. Do not be intimidated by their approach; all you need to do is to clearly think through the control measures that are required for each of the different risks that can be identified, to make them acceptable. Undertaking risk assessment is good practice in all circumstances as it does provide a structured framework in which to assess the planning and delivery of the event.

FIRST AID

The clearest way of ensuring this is covered is by booking one of the voluntary services such as St John Ambulance or the Red Cross. Their contacts should be in your local phone book. For smaller events it is probably not necessary to have ambulance units in attendance just a small team of foot based first aiders.

CROWD MANAGEMENT

Managing the crowd safely is down to event stewards and barriers, natural or otherwise. It is worth remembering that it can be safer not to use barriers in certain spaces and that this can also be beneficial to the atmosphere you are creating and the relationship between the audience and performers.

Think early on about the numbers you are expecting and how many stewards you will need to provide. You may well be able to recruit these partly from within your own organisation. Be prepared to offer basic training as there is much more to the role than merely having a presence on site.

> For more information on event staff and crowd management…
> See ON THE DAY: Event Staff

POLICE

It is important to highlight the event plan to your local police. They may have a specific officer who deals with liaison for events. Also, the Police are unpredictable in their approach to even smaller e[vents?] they specify that they should have a presence then this may ha[ve a] significant cost (likely to be at least £30 per officer hour), thus it is really important to fully convey to them who the target audience is for the event, for example if it will mostly be families and thus not warranting a major police presence.

LICENSING, PERMISSIONS AND INSURANCE
LICENSING

The Licensing Act 2003 received royal assent in July 2003 and the associated *Guidance issued under section 182 of the Licensing Act 2003* in July 2004. [6] This new act replaces all previous licensing legislation in respect of alcohol and public entertainment in England and Wales. At the time of writing the First Appointed Day, at which the system starts to change, is approaching in February 2005, with the Second Appointed Day, when the changes have to have been made, following nine months later in November.

The Government's aim with the new legislation is to make the processes of licensing easier and ensure a light touch approach and consistency throughout England and Wales. The Act safeguards four main objectives: prevention of public nuisance; public safety; prevention of crime and prevention of harm to children. The majority of the legislation is concerned with alcohol supply and control. If your event is not to include the supply of alcohol then some of the most salient sections to spend more time on are:

In the Act: Part 3 – Premises Licences; Part 5 - Permitted Temporary Activities; Schedule 1 - Provision of Regulated Entertainment.

In the Guidance: Section 5 – Premises Licences; Section 8- Permitted Temporary Activities (Temporary Event Notices); Schedule E - Pool of conditions relating to public safety.

An outdoor free street arts event will need to be presented in an area that has been granted a Premises Licence (unless it is going to be for less than 96 hours and attract an audience of less than 500 at any one time – if this is the case a Temporary Event Notice may be sufficient).

The legislation expressly encourages local authorities to take out Premises Licences themselves on public areas such as town squares, village greens and parks and to allow events to be promoted in these spaces. Do find out if your local authority has done, or is considering doing so. This may make life a little easier for you, though you will still have to operate under the terms of the Licence they have been granted for the particular space. Each local authority is having to consult upon and publish a statement of licensing policy to guide the implementation of the Act. All have been lobbied to make specific reference to street arts and circus provision in these.

More information can be found in the ISAN *Safety Guidance...* and *A Bluffers Guide to the Act* is being jointly created by ISAN, Circus Arts Forum, Equity and Arts Council England, and is available as a free PDF download on the ISAN website from February 2005.

INSURANCE

In this day and age of litigation, insurance and liability are areas that you must not ignore. As an event organiser there are particular policies that can be taken out with companies specialising in this area. ISAN is currently creating a list of the different companies and brokers that are experts in this area of the arts.

It is important that you clearly state the type of event, the activities you will be presenting and the anticipated numbers of audience you will be drawing over the duration of the event. If things change or you suddenly realise that there is a significant amount of knife throwing or flame eating in one of the shows make sure that this is covered in the cover you have. It is standard practice that street arts companies have their own cover as well; this is now normally required to a level of £2-£5 million. This, of course means that the event is doubly insured but this is as much a reflection of the times that we live in. Ask for certificates of Public Liability and risk assessments of your artists' shows with return of contract.

NB. It is very likely that international companies will not carry valid insurances for performances in the UK. You may need to extend your cover for all risks of their show or direct them (with your assistance) to a friendly insurance broker who will allow them to take out a very time limited policy to cover the UK shows.

ROAD CLOSURES

In street arts, one of the great joys of the work is the need, at times, to apply for road closures. This will give you different spaces for presenting work and it can be liberating for the audience to have access to roadways which normally are there for cars and buses. The granting of permission will depend on how important the road is in the locality and the case you can make to your local highways department, who then consult with the emergency services, public transport authorities and other affected parties. When you make an application for road closure can vary from place to place, but it is best to sound out the appropriate persons as early as you can. Road closures do cost and you may also have to pay for signage and security to staff these whilst they are in operation.

The best advice is to locate the appropriate officer and make their acquaintance with the expectation that you will be seeking their advice and making an application in the future.

POWER, STAGING AND EQUIPMENT

Production issues have to be considered in the earliest stages of planning your event. Even for a relatively small-scale event there will be major implications in terms of the resources that are required. These resources may be straightforward budget- related issues such as the hiring in of stages, PA's, etc. However, what must not be underestimated is the amount of planning time it will take.

TECHNICAL REQUIREMENTS

Do try and respect the technical requirements that artists and companies request. If the demands are higher than you can comfortably meet then this should be considered at the point of programming and costed out fully and may result in you not booking that particular company.

POWER

The most often asked for technical requirement will be access to power. Power is often built into street furniture and may be available from lighting poles. You will need to identify who is responsible for the power and how you can get access to it. It is important that groups inform you what sort of connection they require, ideally this should be a waterproof connection such as Cee form. Hiring generators is another way to provide power in the street or on a vehicle. They can be noisy and may need security, so be sensitive where you use them.

PA

Many companies tour with their own PAs these days. Obviously these will require power and you should direct where they are to be set up. With these and other electrical goods you should ensure that the equipment has been properly PAT tested and that you are confident the company looks after their equipment properly.

If you are hiring in a PA then you must ensure that you have an engineer and crew there specifically to set it up and work with it. Even if it is only for playing simple backing tracks for shows, you need someone who is capable of cueing up the CD or Mini-disk and pressing play at the right moments (again something to have double checked with the companies before the day).

STAGING

If you decide to use a small stage for bands at your event you should look at the resource implications of this early on, as it may prove quite costly if you only have modest budgets to play with. An open platform may be sufficient to raise up predominately acoustic groups, but it is worth while seriously considering a covered area, as an open stage is of course susceptible to the vagaries of the weather. If you are working with a PA then this is absolutely to be advised because it can mean that even if it rains in the hours preceding the event, the set up and sound checks can still take place.

In your scheduling you will need to build in the time for change over and sound-checks and line tests on the stage.

For obvious health and safety reasons it is important that a certified supplier supplies you with this small staging. They must be able to supply the engineering calculations on the stage and any cover, particularly relating to construction, point loadings and how the thing is anchored down in winds. The staging supplier should sign off the stage that it has been erected to its normal standards.

MARKETING AND PRESS

As most general event organisers will already be significantly involved in a great deal of marketing and press within their jobs, these notes only focus on specific points relating to street arts events.

MARKETING

Don't make the mistake of thinking that because the event is free people will come. Marketing is vital to achieve a mix of people. Don't also assume that just because people are in town to shop that they will generate the right atmosphere and provide all of the audience you desire on their own. In the ISAN / City University research, 62% of those interviewed had made a special trip to be at the event. It is highly advantageous to have people there who have come specially to watch and take part – they act to encourage others to stop too.

Marketing needs to be considered in the same way as for other events. If you are aiming for a wider audience than arts attendees, you will need to produce print and more - it is worth pointing out that leaflets are picked up much less often by non-artsgoers. Street branding and radio are more likely to attract a wider variety of the public.

Street branding - banners hanging over balconies in the local shopping centre, or across the front of your civic building, or lamppost pennants - is always effective. However it is expensive, requires you to have a good - and preferably free - relationship with your street lighting department and will need to be covered in your risk assessment unless you are using standard council facilities.

Radio advertising can, again, be expensive, but you can sometimes get cheaper radio slots - and newspaper advertising - if you offer a competition. This works well if you can give away tickets to other events in your programme or prizes from shops and restaurants in the locality of the event.

Print should clearly state that the event is FREE (if it is). The visual impact of street arts means it is sensible to produce a full colour leaflet. Many performers have good photographs you can use and you should also begin to build up your own library of photographs of your events. You may find posters are a good vehicle if you can persuade local shops, cafés, etc. to display them.

PRESS

It is not difficult to get a limited amount of advance coverage in regional press, although it can sometimes be rather focused on the bizarre or condescending.

Press releases should concentrate on the following in order to get the kind of coverage you really want:

→ Street arts are of high quality, engaging, fascinating and eye-opening. You could be brave and use more "arts language" if you know your journalist.

→ An excellent atmosphere will be generated in town - your festival makes the most of the recent regeneration / new plaza / pedestrianisation, etc.

→ Uniqueness, special artists - international if you have them - or premieres (journalists do take an interest in uniqueness). Highlight these.

→ The benefits to the local economy - both shopping and artists.

→ Street festivals are for everyone - one of the few art forms that appeal to several generations at the same time.

→ A lively, colourful and infectiously joyous afternoon – an important feel-good factor in these contemporary stressful times.

To get more than one article or picture before your event, some of these may help:

→ Try and set up a photo call and/or an interview with a local street company or a community arts project being undertaken for your festival with a local group.

→ Choose one excellent photograph of one of your groups and duplicate (as a high resolution Jpeg as well as a hard print version) and copy it to all journalists and picture editors if such a thing exist on the local paper. They may well use it. Remember that (unfortunately for us!) journalists prefer pictures without crowds in.

→ They also love dramatic poses - but remember they will often go for children on stilts or a red nosed clown if you give them half a chance, so make sure you positively guide the photographer to the best possible image.

→ Spoon feed press releases on all artists - try and keep them as short and pithy as possible - they may use them in their entirety. A difficulty with street festivals is that there are often lots of artists, so it's easier for journalists to focus on a stilt walker or colourful clown unless you guide them.

→ It can be a great help to find a local shopkeeper, publican, or suchlike, who is enthusiastic and introduce your journalist to him/her. They can then cover your story but from a different angle.

For details of how to get the best press coverage of the event day itself…
See *ON THE DAY: Press*

PICTURE 07

CASE STUDY 3: EALING SUMMER STREETS
Pam McCrea, Ealing Borough Council Festival and Events Team

THE EVENT
Ealing Summer Streets forms one part of the Ealing Summer Festival Programme, a series of festivals produced by Ealing Borough Council Festivals and Events over July and August. This includes:

Ealing Jazz Festival – 7 days
Ealing Blues Festival – 1 day
Ealing Comedy Festival – 6 nights
Ealing Summer Classical Concert – 1 day
The London Mela – 1 day

Ealing Summer Streets began as a one day event in 2003. The festival has to work within the parameters of its small budget and the available sites which are suitable for the size of audience, but there is a strong belief in the importance of presenting street arts. The underlying reason for this is that it introduces the existing festival audience to a different art form and through diversifying the programme, also attracts a new and wider audience. The Summer Streets programme is designed to be adventurous but also very accessible to a family audience.

The festival takes place over three sites: Ealing Green W5, Ealing Broadway Centre W5 (both in Ealing Town Centre) and Leeland Road, West Ealing, W13. It was decided to include static and walkabout performance as well as a larger scale finale piece from an International company. The first year's programme, therefore, included walkabout from Pear Shape Performance and Original Mixture, music from the Ding Dong Daddios and static work from The Chipolatas, The Invisible Men, Dot Comedy and Swizzleshaker, which mixed theatre, visual comedy and circus.

The finale show was from German Company Scharlatan Theater who brought a spoof fire brigade to create comedy theatre with fire and water effects, fire engines and pyrotechnics. The show also involved the local Ealing Fire Brigade coming to put out a (controlled) fire as a comic end to the piece. There was a desire to introduce audiences to larger scale international work and to have a visually spectacular finale piece as part of the festival. This was made more affordable by sharing travel and accommodation costs with Stockton International Riverside Festival and the company also offered a good price as they were already touring in England.

In order to develop the programme of Ealing Summer Streets, the festival aims to work collaboratively with other organisations to co-commission new work and to increase opportunities of booking more international companies by sharing costs (something which ISAN members often do amongst themselves and with others). There is a belief that commissioning new work provides supportive opportunities for artists and helps to further develop this type of work. The festival is also interested in developing specific opportunities for new work from culturally diverse British based artists working in street arts. There is also the intention to make use of the participatory nature of street arts to provide access for local community involvement in the Festival

THE LOCAL SITUATION
Stakeholders of Ealing Festival include local businesses, town centre management and local organisations such as Ealing Centre Partnership. It is important for the festival to understand and promote the wider potential benefits on a local level, for example, by giving a taster of how street arts can be incorporated into a town centre and regeneration strategy to enhance an area. Social benefits, such as community involvement in the festival, run alongside economic benefits, such as the increased income for local businesses because of the number of people in the area, and the chance to establish sponsorship relationships with local businesses.

BUDGET BREAKDOWN
Income – where does the money come from?
Total Budget £10,000
→ London Borough of Ealing Festival and Events core budget.
→ London Borough of Ealing Regeneration (strategically – this was on the basis that the street arts event would contribute to help the development of the West Ealing area – the Leeland Road performance site was in this area and the acts occurred while the farmers market was operating).
→ Ealing Broadway Shopping Centre – One of the sites is in the shopping centre square.
→ Income from French Market on one of the Street arts sites (Ealing Green) which took place during the event.

Expenditure - where does it go?	%
→ artistic	75
→ staff	15
→ production / tech	10

Production costs were low for 2003, due to the nature of the performance programmed. Most needed very little technical production and were self sufficient. Dressing rooms were sourced free of charge and power was taken from mains supply, without a charge. The festival was able provide its own equipment, such as tables, fire extinguishers, gazebos etc. Two small PAs were hired. Summer Streets was marketed as part of Ealing Council's wider events programme. The marketing did not, therefore, impact on this budget.

WHY DOES IT WORK?

The first ever Ealing Summer Streets was blessed with a fantastic, responsive audience, in spite of the bad weather! The nature of this type of performance is that it has wide appeal and is accessible to a diverse audience. Spreading the work over three sites led to it being seen by more people and using the Ealing Broadway shopping centre as one of these sites meant a captive audience within. Combining the festival with a French Market and a Farmers' market created a more vibrant street atmosphere which worked well for the event as a whole.

Being part of a larger festival programme meant the marketing was well presented, efficiently distributed and effective in drawing the audience to a new event. The audience then stayed and were appreciative because of the quality of the programme of work on offer. This and the fact that the event was well organised and managed are mainly due to the prior knowledge and experience of the programmer and event staff.

PICTURE 08

ON THE DAY

SETTING UP / RIGGING

Realistically work out how much time and how many members of staff you will need to put the site together. This includes:

Signage

Barriers

Power

Staging / structures / marquees

Technical set up and checks

It is better to build in extra time in case of unforeseen difficulties.

Make sure all contractors are aware of your schedule and know when to arrive and who to report to. If you do have to set up the day before, make sure you can secure the site overnight.

EVENT STAFF

CORE TEAM

If possible, organise your team so that you have one named person (not you!) who has responsibility for each of the different aspects (production, artists, steward coordination, etc.). If you invest responsibility in your programme and production team, this means you are free to deal with any unforeseen circumstances, while somebody else can confidently make a decision about whether that stage needs to move three feet to the right. This way you might actually also see some of the work, the audience reactions and the atmosphere of the event as it changes over the day. This is all valuable for your own evaluation of the event. Make sure you talk to some of your audience members and that your team and stewards do too. Informal feedback can tell you much more than a multiple choice survey.

STEWARDS AND SECURITY

Roles

→ Crowd management: e.g., keeping an eye on the public at key areas such as crush points; steering the audience along a specified route and so on.

→ Artist support: helping artists arrive, collect passes, find dressing rooms and leave

→ Accompanying strolling performers

→ Site / stage management: being on duty at a specific site.

→ Front of House: selling programmes, running the information stand.

Most street arts events differentiate between official security staff, who may be bought in from an external company, and their own stewards. Bought in security staff should be licensed and trained to manage entry and egress points and to handle minor disturbances. Your stewards may be paid or volunteers, but at least some of the roles mentioned above would require people with experience or training. Ask other staff in your organisation if they would like to be stewards - they may enjoy the event and the opportunity for overtime or time off in lieu it may present. It is also beneficial to have stewards who have some degree of background information so that they can talk confidently with the audience. There are definite cons to working with volunteers unless you have existing strong relationships with individuals who can be trusted to turn up on the day and have the maturity to take on the important roles that stewards do fulfil.

Brief all staff verbally and provide them with briefing notes covering emergency procedures (including any codes), communications information, critical timings and any other information they might need.

For example steward briefing notes…
See *APPENDIX 2*

EVENT CONTROL / COMMUNICATIONS

Though you are not planning a major event it is good practice to have a nominated centre of operations where the base for communications is and which is staffed at all times. This may be useful situated adjacent to where the artists and stewards are based.

A radio system should be hired in for the day to ensure clear and easy communication between the main event organiser the artists' dressing room area and the various key stewards of the different areas as well as services such as information points and first aid. Make sure everybody knows how to use the radios correctly and clearly, including whether you are using different channels. Have a brief list of code words to use when reporting emergencies such as a disturbance, or a fire, in order to avoid panicking the crowd.

HEALTH AND SAFETY

You will need to do final checks against your safety plan and risk assessment, ensuring that any measures to reduce risk have been put in place. A health and safety officer may wish to accompany you on a tour of the site to ensure that they are also satisfied with the set up.

You will need to hire in fire fighting equipment and a hire company will be able to advise on which type of fire extinguishers and how many you will need when given details of your event.

Ensure that your first aid station is clearly visible and there is signage to indicate where it can be found.

Brief all staff carefully on any evacuation procedures and how they will be alerted if these should need to be put into action.

Again, for greater detail on health and safety…
See *Safety Guidance for Street Arts, Carnival, Procession and Large-Scale Performances* (ISAN 2004)

PERFORMERS

If you get nothing else right, make it easy for the performers to find the site and to park nearby. They will thank you for this. Performing outdoors can be stressful at best and this is not helped by trying to find a parking space in an unfamiliar town centre. It is also essential to provide performers with secure dressing rooms and some refreshments. A separate green room for the latter is desirable.

Make sure you have all the technical provision requested by the performers, including a technician to operate this if the company does not have their own.

Shows should be provided with an adequate number of stewards. This includes walkabout acts who are often more comfortable with a steward to accompany them. Saturday afternoons in a shopping centre are not the easiest places for certain acts. Someone keeping a discreet eye on how things develop is usually a good idea. It does no one any good to witness a costumed character being pulled about by

some tearaways and can be easily avoided. Most groups have techniques to avoid such attention but even so it does not mean that act is bad if they attract that sort of trouble - It can and does happen to everyone.

WET WEATHER AND OTHER CONTINGENCIES

It is not always possible, but a wet weather alternative should be considered. Artists will often perform in a certain level of rain but after a while it just becomes ridiculous and can seriously damage costumes and props, which have to be reused day in day out through the main touring periods. Some promoters are not sensitive to this and just want their money's worth no matter how wet and how pitiful the act looks or how empty the street is. It is important for there to have been proper discussion between artists and promoters to decide what is possible in these situations.

PUBLIC INFORMATION

An information point is useful on many levels. Obviously the audience will be grateful for a place to find out about performance times, site locations and any other queries they may have. If there are any last minute changes to the programme then these information sources should be informed. On another level, it gives you a direct contact with your audience and can be a means of letting them know more about you and the work you do.

You may need to produce a simple piece of print with a specific schedule for distribution on the day. A programme of what is on when and where will keep people longer and encourage them to move around looking for shows and plan their afternoon. This need not be elaborate - a photocopied sheet will do if you are short of money.

If you are utilising a number of set sites for fixed shows then having boards with a clear running order and times can be helpful for the audience. Such measures as these may not increase the audience numbers but should help in making the ones that you have stay for longer and be more attentive of what is going on.

PRESS

On the day you may well want to get press coverage of your event. Be aware that many journalists equate street arts with busking, with overtones of it being slightly illegal and probably poor quality as otherwise it would be presented somewhere more salubrious than the street. Journalists prefer to write simplistic copy about 'entertaining the kids' and may use words like 'wacky' or 'quirky' with ease.

Regional/local press will usually be more than happy to cover your event, although it may be trivialised. If you can possibly afford to have someone walk round with your journalist/photographer, you can make sure they see the good (and photogenic) groups.

It is very difficult to get national press coverage, even for larger festivals. Unless you are holding a prestigious premiere, or there are other current, newsworthy things about your town that your event provides a link to, your energies may be better spent elsewhere. You may be able to get a photograph taken and printed if you know a freelance photographer who sells into the national press or you've got a really good idea for a picture that is genuinely unique.

DOCUMENTATION AND EVALUATION

Street arts depends on the visual, therefore it is a very good idea to get a photographer to document your event. Give them guidance on the range of images you will need whether this is for reports, future marketing or funding application or for your website.

Getting facts and figures on your audience can be slightly less straightforward than for your average ticketed event. It is possible to 'see' just how large the crowds are and to assess the composition of our audiences in terms of age range or types of groups such as family groups, or a culturally diverse crowd. Possibly an 'independent' source such as the Town Centre Manager or Police may be able to provide you with this information, that may be more easily believed. Other related data, such as hotel room figures, can be used to assess the balance of attendance from those outside the region. Another method of collecting information includes surveying people. Your audience will be more willing to take part if you offer an incentive, such as entering their details in a free prize draw. Of course, the usual Data Protection considerations apply.

For an example audience survey see...
APPENDIX 3

The atmosphere of the crowd is the best guide to the success and quality of events, so make sure you mingle and talk to people.

DE-RIGGING

Make sure that you have every body you can muster to sweep your site for litter at the end of the event. Also make sure that you include yourself in the responsibility to do this. If you are operating in a park, it may be that there are staff to do this (although you may be liable to pay them an extra fee because of the increased volume of litter).

After this there will still be plenty of jobs for volunteers as well as those which needs to be done by trained people, i.e. staging, marquees and so on. Make sure somebody walks the site to pick up any props or pieces of kit that performers may have left behind. If you are keeping kit overnight for performers or suppliers, make sure that it is secure until it will be collected.

AFTER THE EVENT
DEBRIEF

As soon as possible after the event, arrange debrief sessions with your staff, your original consultation/planning group and other parties that had input into the event. You may choose to talk to the different groups separately or all around one table. Talk through how the experience was for them and whether it met their expectations and be prepared to take on board some of their comments for future events.

Also consider the feedback you gathered from your audience, local residents and community participants. Check the local papers afterwards for reviews or letters about your event (although remember that people are perhaps more inclined to act if they have a negative response than a positive one and don't take this as the final word on public opinion). Feedback from local businesses can also be valuable. At this stage, when the comments are fresh, it is a beneficial process to consider how you would pay heed to these views in your future planning.

KISSPENSARY

Specials
-Sweet Kiss
-Tattoo Kiss
-Goodluck Kiss
-Christmas Kiss
-Secret Kiss
-Butterfly Kiss
-Alien Kiss
ADVICE
*New from the Kiss
Therapy Research
Centre:
Test Your Pucker*

PICTURE 09

Most importantly, you should revisit your own original vision for the event and think about whether it did actually meet this. The other parties involved will have strong views on specific aspects, but it is likely that you will have the only truly overall picture.

This is now also the time when you will need to complete any reports or evaluation required by your funders.

"WRAP" PARTY

The reality of festival work is that lots of people give a great deal of their time and energy to ensure the event is a success. Try to provide an opportunity to thank your staff and volunteers. This could be combined with the debrief sessions as a sweetener!

NEXT YEAR

…can wait! Now you get to go on holiday when everyone else is back at work…and if that holiday can include visiting other festivals to see the work on offer there, then all the better!

CASE STUDY 4: SLOUGH ARTS ALIVE
Karen Poley, Project Producer Zap Art

PICTURE 10a

PICTURE 10b

PICTURE 10c

THE EVENT

Slough Arts Alive is a free, annual festival of street arts, which takes place in the streets of Slough town centre in July. In 2004 the event celebrated its 10th anniversary. This Slough Borough Council event is produced by Zap Art working in partnership with local artists, arts groups and Creative Partnerships.

The programme seeks to combine a range of high quality, culturally diverse professional artists; local performing arts community groups and local and regionally based visual and craft artists who undertake workshops on site. In 2003 and 2004, Arts Alive has undertaken extensive educational workshops in local schools, with Creative Partnerships, which have led to performances by school children at the event.

Over the years, Arts Alive has commissioned professional and local artists to produce new street arts performances and visual decorations for the performance spaces. The Festival has regularly undertaken street arts workshops and masterclasses for local groups to develop awareness of street arts and interest in the genre amongst local audiences.

THE LOCAL SITUATION

Key ambitions for the event are to involve the range of Slough's culturally diverse communities and to encourage the development of street arts in the area.

The event has sought to appeal to the widest range of audiences

through presenting high quality performances, involving local artists, educational opportunities and audience development. The event takes place in Slough High Street providing a familiar setting for local people to see a diverse range of performances.

In terms of booking professional street artists, we aim to include as wide a range as possible of very high quality work. There are few professional street artists from culturally diverse backgrounds, which limits programming options. However, we always look to include at least one company, such as High Flyers or Nutkhut as well as work from Slough, if possible, and also tend towards culturally non-specific work, such as The Freds or Electric Cabaret.

Arts Alive has always encouraged local groups to perform at the event. This obviously develops artist and audience links with local communities, increases the cultural breadth of the event relevant to the local population and increases local ownership of the event. Many local groups aren't necessarily performers, so we've looked at other ways to involve local people, for example, through the on site workshop programme as both artists and participants. In 2004 Rakhi workshops, African-Caribbean braiding, Arabic Calligraphy, Bollywood Dance and Cuban Dance workshops took place, amongst others. We have also looked to encourage local people to produce street arts performances themselves through direct commissioning, street arts workshops with specific groups and developing street arts skills through masterclasses for local professional and amateur artists.

Street arts residencies in schools has been a major element of the programme in the last two years. Working with Creative Partnerships we have sought to extend awareness of the range and level of street arts by seeking to bring it into the curriculum of local schools. Within the context of a residency to create a street arts performance for Arts Alive, school children have learnt about working as a team, developing new skills and confidence and play in a creative and focused way. With careful programming we have seen excellent performances including Javanese horse dancing, body percussion, stunning 'live art' representations of famous artworks and highly developed physical comedy walkabouts.

BUDGET BREAKDOWN

Income - where does the money come from?

Income comes from a range of sources including:

→ Local Authority
→ Sponsorship
→ Creative Partnerships
→ Grants from ACE

Expenditure - where does it go?   %

→ artistic programme   50
  including the large education programme.

→ technical / production   10
  quite low which reflects a programming ethos to avoid technically heavy performances, and also that there is no evening production.

→ staffing   35
  reflecting the high level of educational work and the event's developmental activities.

→ marketing   5
  low this year (2004) as a result of sharing publicity with another event taking place in the area on the same weekend. Event posters were placed throughout the town by the Borough Council whose PR department also liaised with local media.

WHY DOES IT WORK?

In its 10th year, Arts Alive is well established in Slough's annual calendar of events. The key to its success has been involving local people and organisations, developing links and relationships and introducing them to street arts through careful programming and scheduling. This year, for example, over 250 local school children took part in educational projects in 6 schools and approximately 175 participated on the day. Imagine how many parents, brothers, sisters, aunties, uncles, grandmothers, etc. they bring along with them. Alongside the efforts of their children, they are invited to watch entertainment as well as more challenging and difficult performances and try out an art or craft activity from other cultures.

Slough Borough Council is an extremely supportive partner, which has always viewed Arts Alive from a wider, strategic perspective, as part of its regeneration programme. In 2004, in particular, this enabled a number of organisations working with the Council to link up in a mutually beneficial way and enhance the Arts Alive programme. For example, Arts Alive shared print material and some programme with another local event, Dance in the Park, held on the following day. In addition, Art in the Centre, an initiative to revitalise Slough High Street, commissioned visual artworks for the event.

Through our second major partner, Creative Partnerships, Arts Alive potentially has access to the hearts and minds of teachers and pupils across the borough and beyond and also to other partners. Posters for the event were distributed to teachers and local schools throughout the area. In addition, the Festival linked up with the WOMAD Foundation in a Cuban dance and music project. This enabled Arts Alive to present high quality papier mache Carnival costumes by Cuban artists, the Mora Brothers and pupils from Langleywood School as part of the event finale.

Last but not least, Arts Alive works with extremely helpful and supportive friends in the community; everyone from local security officers to car park attendants and curates from local churches. Many people are genuinely delighted to help and make the event work. Without their input the atmosphere would just not be the same and the event would not be as successful.

APPENDIX 1: EXAMPLE CONTRACT FOR ARTISTS

An agreement is made between: _____ (Known hereafter as the management)

And: _____ (Known hereafter as the artist/s)

Witness that the management hereby engages and the artist/s accept the engagement:

Type of performance: _____

Event: _____

Date: _____

Venue: _____

Performance time: _____

No. of shows: _____

Duration of shows: _____

It is agreed that the fee is: _____

Plus travel: _____

Plus VAT: _____

Total Fee: _____

Cheque made payable to: _____ to be issued no more than two weeks after the date of the performance.

The management will provide:

- Clear directions and a map to be sent at least two weeks before the performance date
- Any necessary passes
- Parking facilities giving a good access to performance site
- Secure changing facilities
- Light refreshments
- Adequate security where necessary to ensure safety of performers
- Technical requirements

The artist/s will provide:

- Evidence of current liability insurance
- Publicity material to be sent on request from the management
- Full information of technical requirements sent at least one month before the performance date.

In the event of bad weather or other circumstances beyond the artist's control, the fee will remain payable.

APPENDIX 2: EXAMPLE BRIEFING NOTES FOR STEWARDS

Thank you for joining the event team today. The work involves looking after sites where performances are happening, helping out with artists, audience and stage crews where necessary, selling programmes, giving out information, trouble shooting, clearing up at the end and anything else that needs doing! Everyone mucks in – festival directors, crew and volunteers.

Enjoy yourself! Remember you are the first point of contact for the public so how you come across is the image they will take away of the festival organisation. Make sure you are well informed or can direct members of the public to where they can get further information. Do talk to people and, if you can, get feedback on their feelings about the day, their favourite groups and so on.

Stewards / site workers are key personnel on event days.

- The main role of a steward / site worker is to make things flow easily and without problems in the area you are working.

- To do this effectively you will need to:

  - Know who is managing your site overall. In particular, check who on your site is in radio contact with the festival organisation.

  - Know if there is a technician and who they are.

  - Keep aware of the stage area and who is in it – keeping people away who should not be in it.

  - Keep aware of artists who might need you for something.

  - Know where the dressing rooms are for the artists at your site.

  - Be aware of the timing of the programme and try to run your site on time.

  - Know where all the other festival sites are.

  - Be aware of any members of the audience who may need assistance.

  - Know where the lost children / first aid areas are.

- Resolve any problems that arise yourself if you can. If not, use the person with radio contact (or radio through yourself if you have one) to get assistance from another part of the site.

- Each site should have a clear schedule of running times, any technical changes that need to be made, barriers moving etc. Make sure you know where this will be so you can consult it.

- Problems with performers:

  - the only likely problem is lateness! Make sure someone on your site team goes to collect artists in enough time so that they are ready to start 5 minutes before their scheduled time.

- Problems with the audience:

  - deal with people's enquiries in as enthusiastic a way as you can. Excitement about the day is infectious. You can often sidestep people's anxieties by being friendly and cooperative.

    be as courteous as possible when asking the audience to move back or not go onto the stage area. "Please" and "thank you" work wonders with potentially aggressive people of all ages.

  - try not to get angry with people. If you feel you are losing your calm, call your site manager to help out. This is not a failure. Sometimes two people are better than one.

- Don't be too anxious if things run late or have to change or if there are technical problems. We'll all try hard to avoid these, but at events like this they do happen.

- At the end of the day, make sure your site is clear of equipment, props and so on. Artists may need some help with their gear. Make sure there is always someone from the team on site if anything valuable has been left there.

- Last of all, we will all need to litter pick all areas before we leave the site. Bin bags are provided – it usually takes half an hour.

- Emergencies. Make sure you have been briefed on what to do in case of emergency, in particular, how to report the emergency and where to evacuate the site to. If in doubt, call a festival organiser on the radio.

Thank you!

FURTHER READING

THE PRACTICALITIES

Code of Practice for the Engagement of Artists (ISAN 2002).
Available as a download at www.streetartsnetwork.org.uk
All ISAN members sign up to this code of practice which also offers a benchmark for non-members to operate to.

The Event Safety Guide (HSE, 1999) ISBN 0-7176245-3-6.
Available from www.hsebooks.co.uk or tel: 01787 88 11 65
The "Purple Book" brings together information needed by events organisers, their contractors and employees to help them satisfy the requirements of the Health and Safety at Work Act 1974 and associated regulations. It enables organisers to understand the needs of others concerned with events, such as local authorities and emergency services. The HSE also endorse ISAN's publication *Safety Guidance for Street Arts, Carnival, Processions and Large-Scale Performance* (see opposite) as a companion to this book.

Festivals Mean Business (BAFA, 2001).
Available from BAFA (British Arts Festivals Association)
www.artsfestivals.co.uk or tel: 0207 247 4667
This was the first nationwide study of festivals since 1992, providing new financial coordinates for the arts festivals scene, and examining the cultural, social and economic impact of arts festivals in the UK. The original report was given an update in December 2002 to provides yet further evidence of the strength of British Arts Festivals, and the continued impact they have across the UK.

Strategy and Report on Street Arts (Arts Council England, 2002)
ISBN 0-7287-0867-1. Available as a download on
www.artscouncil.org.uk

The Licensing Act 2003 Available from www.hmso.gov.uk
The new act which replaces all previous licensing legislation in respect of alcohol and public entertainment in England and Wales. It is also appropriate to read the associated guidance:
Guidance issued under section 182 of the Licensing Act 2003.
Available from www.culture.gov.uk

THE PRACTICE

Cafagna, Giovanni *The Gig* (Giovanni Cafagna –
Peter Parker Media, 2002) ISBN 0-9541972-0-8.
A photographic essay on British street theatre, performed by Strangelings.

Herrmann, Paul et. al. *Playing with Fire*
(Manchester International Arts, 2000) ISBN 0-9537981-0-0
See www.streetsahead.org.uk for details of how to buy.
A beautiful photograph book of the Streets Ahead festival held in Manchester 1995-1999. The book has four essays from the perspective of the artist, the organiser, the photographer and the audience member, giving valuable insight into the documenting of a major popular festival. Paul Herrmann's photography perfectly captures the mood of the best street arts events.

Coult, Tony and Kershaw, Baz *Engineers of the Imagination* (Methuen, 1982. Revised 1990) ISBN 0-4135280-0-6
See www.welfare-state.org for details of how to obtain a copy.
A book to get thumbmarks and glue on, as it explains the basic techniques of Welfare State International's work – the making of processions; large scale puppets; fixed structures; fire and ice technology; processional, theatre and dance music, celebratory food and feasts and much more.

Fox, John *Eyes on Stalks* (Methuen, 2002) ISBN 0-4137649-0-8
See www.welfare-state.org for details of how to obtain a copy.
An autobiographical roller coaster through three decades of wild inventions, Eyes on Stalks covers the principals and practice of site specific theatre, extensive community residencies and new rites of passage. This is a mixture of personal stories, clear instructions, scripts and poems, lavishly illustrated with 30 photographs and over 100 drawings from John Fox's sketch book.

Mason, Bim *Street Theatre and Other Outdoor Performance*
(Routledge, 1992) ISBN 0-4150705-0-3 Out of print.
Contact bigheadbim@aol.com to request an electronic version.
This book is a description, a celebration and an analysis of outdoor theatre, which demonstrates just what a sophisticated art form it is. It provides a practical guide to those who are new to the subject and gives practising performers a new insight on their own work.